I'm glad he is safe with an owner like you

Is Nubs like the amazing dog in the whole world!

♡ your best friend

are very brave.

I'm glad that you helped Nubs.

P.S. you are a kind man.

To the Marines of BTT 3/5/2 —B.D.

To my Beloved, who discovered Nubs's story —M.N.

For Mary, "a true friend and a good writer" —K.L.

Text copyright © 2009 by Major Brian Dennis, Mary Nethery, and Kirby Larson ▪ Front cover photograph and photographs on pages 42 and 45 © 2007 by Karen Maze/www.karenmaze.com ▪ Photographs on page 36 (left-hand side) © 2007 by Denis Poroy ▪ Photographs on page 36 (right-hand side) © 2007 Patty Ducey-Brooks/Presidio Communications ▪ Photographs on pages 38, 39, 43 © 2007 Scott Linnett/*The San Diego Union-Tribune*/ZUMA Press ▪ Photograph on page 40 © 2007 *The Tampa Tribune*. Reprinted with permission.

Special thanks to the following people, who contributed photographs for inclusion in the book: Alicia Cellana, Chrissy Sjoberg, Eric Sjoberg and the Marines in Unit 3/5/2: Capt Alexander Roloff; Capt Ronald A. Hess; 1st Lt Jaime Hinojosa; 1st Lt James Schmidt; MGySgt Donald Hatch; GySgt Wayne Jackson; GySgt Sean Walters; GySgt Patrick Keith; SSgt Joseph Palomo; HM1 Florencio Masadao. Additional thanks to Ms. Kettler's second grade class at Murray Manor Elementary School.

First Edition: November 2009

Library of Congress Cataloging-in-Publication Data

Dennis, Brian, 1971-
  Nubs : the true story of a mutt, a marine & a miracle / by Brian Dennis, Kirby Larson, and Mary Nethery.
    p. cm.
  ISBN 978-0-316-05318-1
  1. Dogs—Iraq—Juvenile literature. 2. Dog owners—California—Juvenile literature. 3. Iraq War, 2003—Personal narratives, American—Juvenile literature. I. Larson, Kirby. II. Nethery, Mary. III. Title.
  SF426.5.D456 2009
  636.7092'9—dc22

                    2009003808

WOR ▪ 10 9 8 7 6 5 4 3 ▪ Printed in the United States of America

The text and display type were set in Glypha ▪ Book design by Liz Casal

Nubs

The True Story of a Mutt, a Marine & a Miracle

MAJOR BRIAN DENNIS ▪ KIRBY LARSON ▪ MARY NETHERY

LITTLE, BROWN AND COMPANY
Books for Young Readers
New York   Boston

Outside a border fort in the desert of western Iraq, a small, thin dog watched and waited. His ears had been cut off to make him a dog of war. He had no name, and no person to call his own.

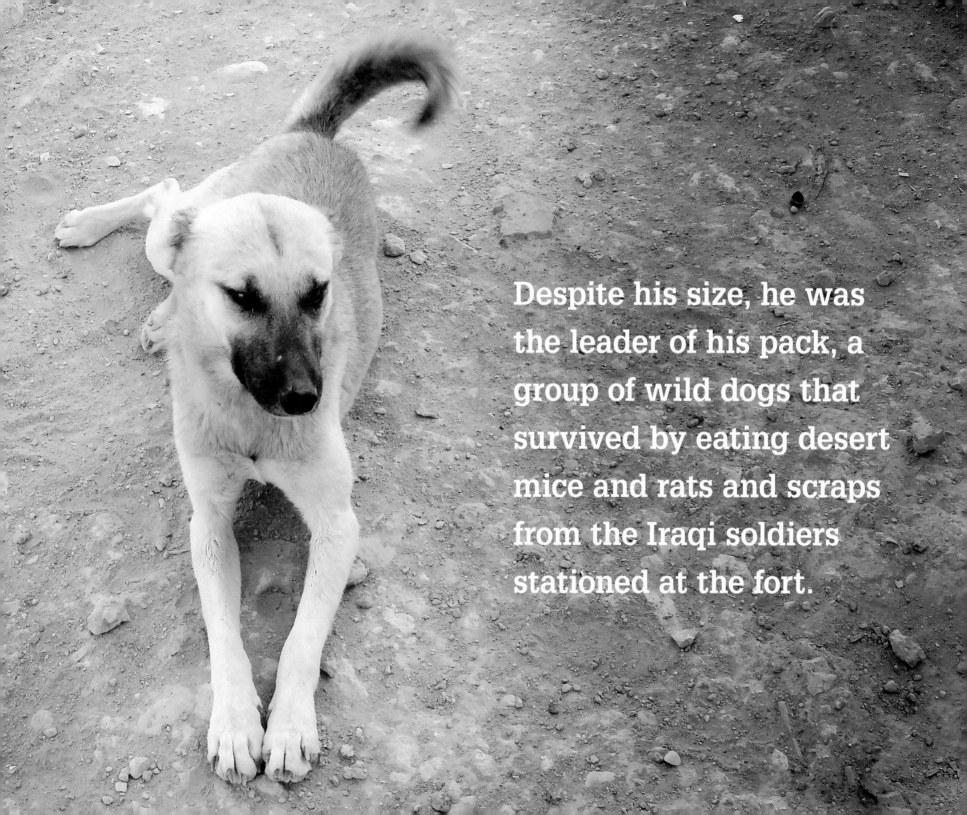

Despite his size, he was the leader of his pack, a group of wild dogs that survived by eating desert mice and rats and scraps from the Iraqi soldiers stationed at the fort.

As the dog scanned the desert for a possible meal, the stillness of the fall morning was broken by the roar of engines, rumbling closer and closer. He hunkered down in the sand.

Three military Humvees, carrying Major Brian Dennis and his ten Marines, lumbered to a stop. They were part of Border Transition Team 3/5/2, there to help train the Iraqi soldiers.

The other pack dogs raced to greet the men.

But the dog without ears cautiously approached Brian, who knelt down on one knee to meet him.

FROM: BRIAN DENNIS
SUBJECT: DESERT DOG
DATE: OCTOBER 2007

I found a dog in the desert. I call him Nubs because his ears look like little "nubs." We clicked right away. He flips on his back and makes me rub his stomach. I taught him to sit and shake in about 5 minutes.

"I call him Nubs because his ears look like little 'nubs.'"

That night, Nubs and Brian ate dinner together.
They shared Brian's MREs—or Meals Ready-to-Eat—
of spaghetti and Cajun beans and rice. For dessert,
Nubs sampled a strawberry Pop-Tart, wagging his tail.

Later that evening, Nubs stayed with Brian when it was
his turn at guard duty. Together they kept everyone safe.

The next day, Brian gave Nubs an extra long belly rub. Then he stepped into his Humvee and drove away.

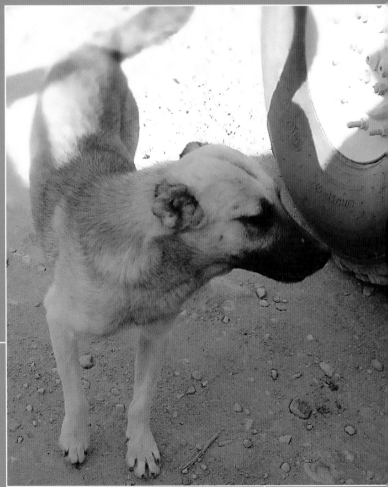

The whole pack chased after the vehicles but quickly lost interest and turned back. Not Nubs. Running faster and faster, he tried to catch up with Brian. He ran for more than a mile. He had no way of knowing that it was against the rules for Marines to have pets.

Left behind, Nubs stared after the Humvees as they disappeared into the shimmering heat of the desert.

Long, lonely weeks passed without any sight of that trio of Humvees the Marines called Scout, Boss, and Chuck.

At the fort, without Brian, there were no belly rubs. Winter's cold winds began to scour the desert, leaving Nubs scrambling for someplace warm to sleep. As the pack leader, he faced constant challenges from younger dogs wanting his job. Sometimes groups of dogs from other forts fought Nubs and his pack over the little food they had. Nubs lived his rough, harsh life waiting for each time Boss carried Brian back to him.

At the fort, without Brian, there were no belly rubs.

FROM: BRIAN DENNIS
SUBJECT: NUBS
DATE: NOVEMBER 2007

On our last trip north I was expecting to see Nubs again. I didn't. We didn't make it as far north as we did last trip, but I still thought I'd see him. I hope that crazy little dog is okay.

Near the end of December, when the temperature dipped to a bone-chilling 30 degrees, the Humvees again rumbled up to the border fort. The pack dogs ran to greet Brian. But not Nubs. He hung back, gaunt and weak from a deep wound in his side.

Shivering from pain, Nubs allowed Brian and the team medic to clean the wound and apply antiseptic ointment from the men's first-aid kits. He even swallowed the child-sized dose of antibiotic Brian gave him. But Nubs refused to eat or drink. It hurt so much, he tried to sleep standing up.

FROM: BRIAN DENNIS
SUBJECT: BAD NEWS
DATE: DECEMBER 2007

We tried to put a blanket on Nubs when we bedded down for the night in the desert, but he wouldn't let us. I said a prayer for him.

He slept near me. It got down to 18 degrees that night and I kept waking up to check on him. Every time I woke up, I wondered if he'd be alive.

When Brian got up at 4 a.m. for his turn at watch, Nubs stiffly padded into place beside him. Head and tail drooping, he faithfully made the rounds with Brian.

The next day, Nubs watched as Brian and his team prepared to leave. He touched his nose to Brian's face as Brian bent down to pet him good-bye. He felt Brian's head on his and heard him whisper, "Hey, buddy, you need to eat. You need to get better."

Then Brian climbed into Boss and the three Humvees pulled away. Determined not to be left behind again, Nubs chased after Brian.

He couldn't keep up.

Alone, he returned to the fort.

NUBS

Two long weeks later, Scout, Boss, and Chuck thundered up to Nubs's fort again. This time Nubs was there to greet them, tail wagging but still moving slowly.

For a few peaceful days, Nubs stuck close to his human "pack." Brian took special care of him, doctoring his wound every morning. Nubs gobbled up his share of Brian's MREs, especially the beef patties. They wrestled and played "give me five." Brian rubbed Nubs's belly every time he asked. If Brian stopped too soon, Nubs pawed him and made him rub some more.

Each night, after the sun set over the desert,
Nubs and Brian did their job together. Under
an ice-black sky of a thousand stars, they
kept watch over everyone.

All too soon, it was time for Brian to leave again. Nubs followed close on his heels. Brian tightened his winter scarf, a Keffiyah, around his neck and then climbed inside the Humvee. He leaned out and said to Nubs, "You take care of yourself, buddy." The vehicles rolled across the desert, slowly at first, then picking up speed, heading for the Command Outpost, far away on the Jordanian border.

Nubs cried as he chased them across the cold, coarse sand. Because of his wound, he could not keep up. He dropped to the ground, exhausted and completely alone.

When Nubs sat up, Scout, Boss, and Chuck were out of sight.
He struggled to his feet and began walking.

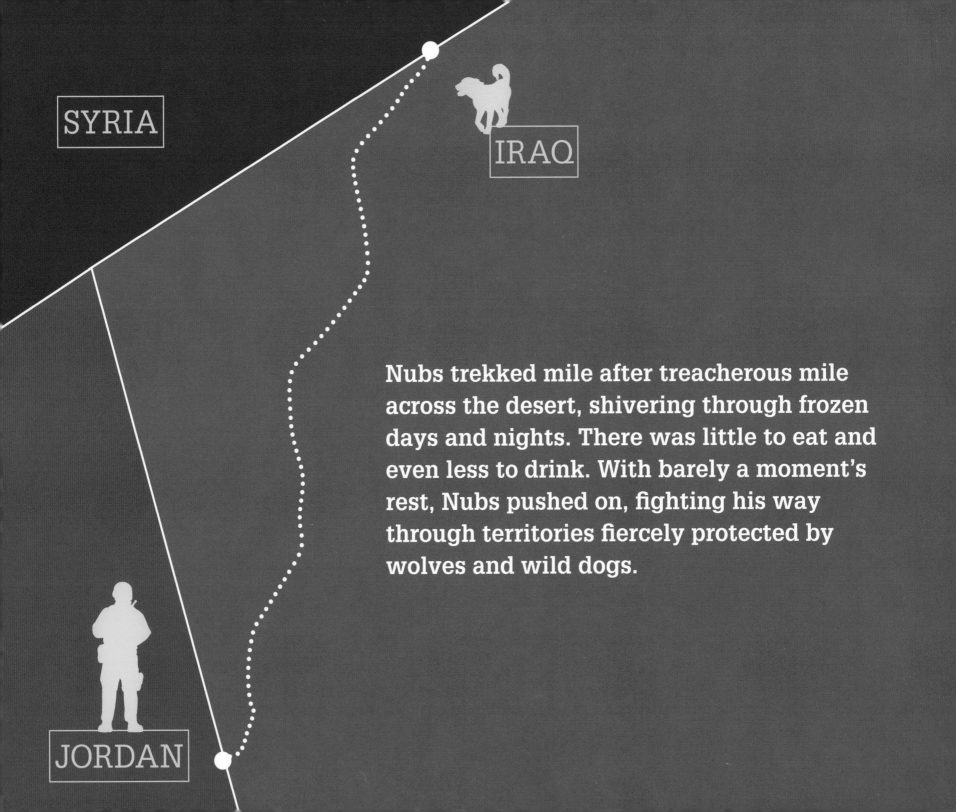

SYRIA

IRAQ

JORDAN

Nubs trekked mile after treacherous mile across the desert, shivering through frozen days and nights. There was little to eat and even less to drink. With barely a moment's rest, Nubs pushed on, fighting his way through territories fiercely protected by wolves and wild dogs.

Two snowy days and 70 miles later, Nubs limped into the Iraqi battalion headquarters, where Brian was working.

A team member ran inside, shouting to Brian, "You're not going to believe who's here!"

"What are you doing here?"

When Nubs saw Brian, he ran with his tongue out and tail wagging, right into his arms.

"What are you doing here?" Brian said as he held Nubs close and rubbed him all over. Nubs finally felt warm again. He pressed his wet nose against Brian's cheek.

Nubs watched Brian climb into Boss, ordering his team back to the Command Outpost just half a mile away.

"I know we're not supposed to have dogs at the outpost," Brian said to his men. "But if he follows us, what can we do?"

When the Humvees began to roll, Nubs trotted right behind them until they reached the Command Outpost.

Starving and exhausted from his ordeal, Nubs wolfed down pancakes, eggs, and sausages the Marines brought him. He made dog-angels, rolling over and over in the freshly fallen snow. A few days later, he found a brand-new doghouse, built just for him.

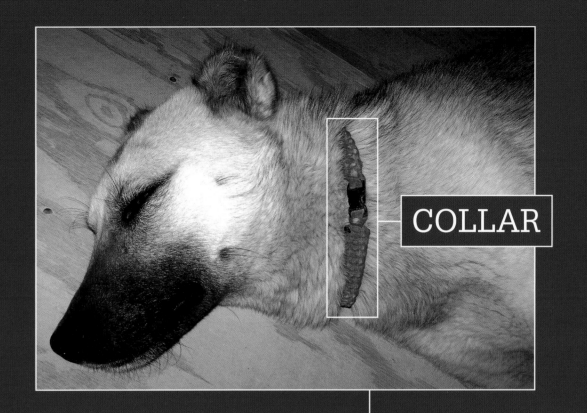

COLLAR

Nubs liked living at the Command Outpost with Brian's men and all the other soldiers. He proudly wore a collar the Marines had fashioned from woven bracelets sent to them from schoolchildren back home. He cheered up his new friends, collecting belly rubs and making them laugh. And, even though he had his own doghouse, most nights Nubs curled up in the barracks with Brian and his team.

But everything was about to change.

"We were given four days to 'get rid of the dog, or else.'"

FROM: BRIAN DENNIS
SUBJECT: NUBS CAN'T STAY
DATE: JANUARY 2008

This all came to a crashing halt when two soldiers, who were not a part of our team, reported us. We were given four days to "get rid of the dog, or else."

That night I sat down and talked to my Marines. We knew that if we took Nubs to the fort he would come back to us. This made the decision easy for me—Nubs was going to America. This dog who had been through a lifetime of fighting, war, and abuse was going to have a nice sunny life and would never be cold again.

Nubs sat close by as Brian e-mailed his family and friends back home, and he supervised the men as they put up flyers to raise the money needed for his journey.

SAVE NUBS FUND!

We are trying to evacuate Nubs to the States via Jordan. It is going to cost upwards of $2,000 to do this. If you want to help "Save Nubs," bring a small cash donation by the BTT 3/5/2 COC. Any bit will help and will be much appreciated. You can even come visit him in San Diego when we get him there. This dog found us after walking nearly 70 miles in the desert and we are going to help him; he is an awesome dog.

UNITED STATES MARINE CORPS
BORDER TRANSITION TEAM 3/5/2
II MARINE EXPEDITIONARY FORCE (FWD)

FROM: BORDER TRANSITION TEAM 3/5/2 TEAM LEADER
TO: JORDANIAN BORDER AUTHORITIES
SUBJ: PASSPORT/TRAVEL DOCUMENT IN THE CASE OF
NUBS DENNIS (A PRIVATELY OWNED DOG BELONGING
TO A U.S. CITIZEN)

1. This paperwork constitutes the passport and travel documentation
for one privately owned dog named Nubs Dennis. He is 2 years old
and weighs 14 KG. Below is his picture. His U.S. identification number
is 323-6371. His final destination will be San Diego, California, United
States of America.

B.P.D.

B.P. DENNIS
MAJ   USMC

Nubs was the first to hear the good news. Family and friends wanted to help!

Nubs posed for his passport photo. He took three baths in three days to get ready for his trip. That was tiring!

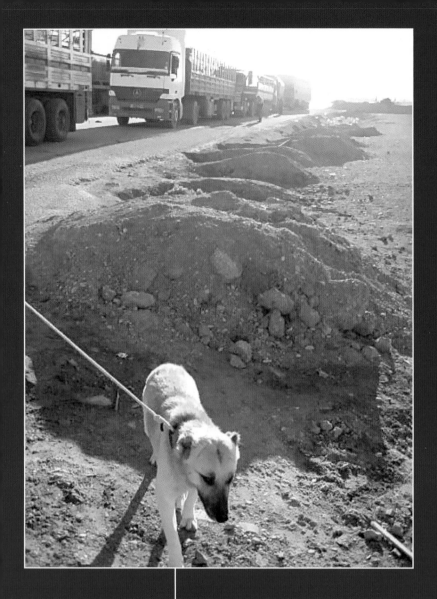

On the last day, Brian packed Nubs's brown blanket and his favorite super-hero toy. Brian made a leash for him out of rope. Nubs didn't play with anyone as he usually did. Instead, he sat quietly in a corner.

When it was time to go, Brian scooped him up and put him in Boss. Together they drove to No Man's Land, the zone between Iraq and Jordan. There, they met the brother of Brian's interpreter, who had agreed to help get Nubs from Jordan to the States. He was escorted by a Jordanian official.

"Be good, buddy."

Nubs rested in Brian's arms as he was carried to a Land Rover. He felt Brian's breath tickle his ear. "Be good, buddy; don't cause any trouble. These guys'll take good care of you. I'll see you in a couple of months. I promise."

Nubs sat at the border checkpoint for hours as officials pored over his paperwork, making sure everything was in order. Finally Nubs arrived in Amman, Jordan. The King of Jordan's veterinarian gave him his first check-up and shots. He stayed at the vet's kennels while his travel was being arranged.

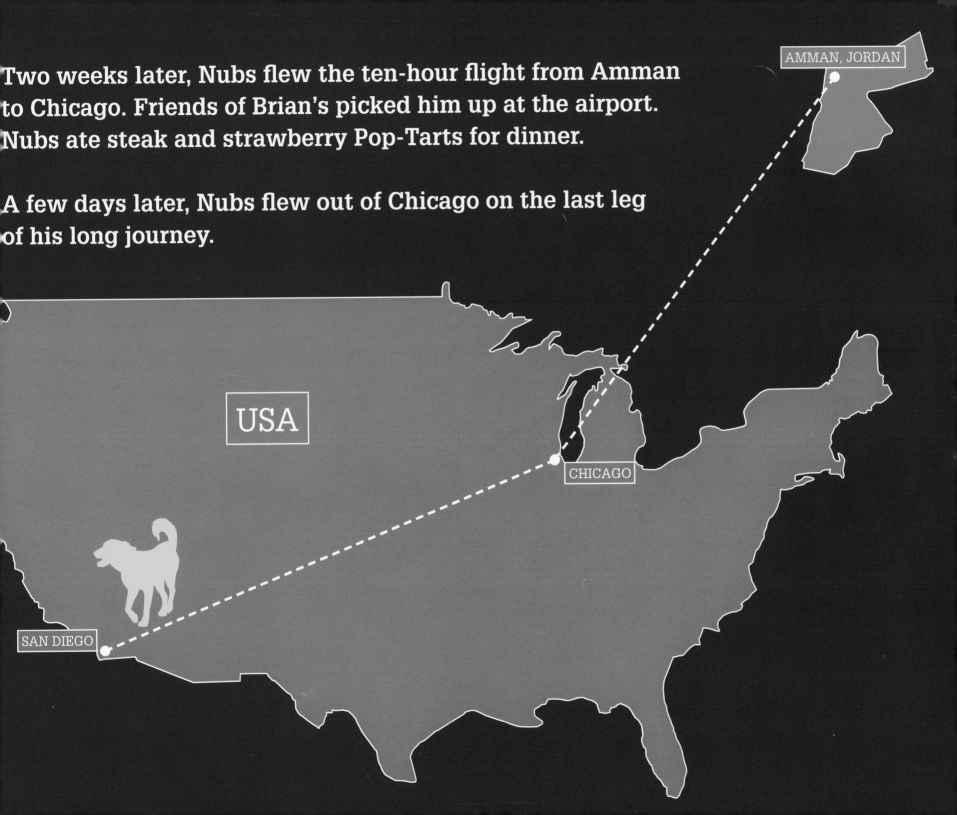

Two weeks later, Nubs flew the ten-hour flight from Amman to Chicago. Friends of Brian's picked him up at the airport. Nubs ate steak and strawberry Pop-Tarts for dinner.

A few days later, Nubs flew out of Chicago on the last leg of his long journey.

AMMAN, JORDAN

USA

CHICAGO

SAN DIEGO

When Nubs stepped off the plane in San Diego, he was greeted with banners and all kinds of cameras. He patiently posed for the "pawparazzi" but was glad to leave the airport crowd with Brian's friends, Eric and Chrissy.

✉ FROM: BRIAN DENNIS
SUBJECT: ROCK STAR NUBS
DATE: FEBRUARY 2008

Well, it's official—Nubs is in San Diego living the good life like a little rock star.

I can't wait to get home and take him to the beach.

Nubs slept in a comfy new dog bed, tried all kinds of tasty food, and went for walks in the dog park.

But someone was missing.

On March 23, 2008, Eric and Chrissy drove Nubs to Camp Pendleton. The "pawparazzi" were there again! Nubs waited and waited. When he finally saw Brian . . .

Nubs leaped into his arms
and covered him with kisses!

Today, Nubs and Brian lead a busy life. They play at the dog beach and cruise around in Brian's truck. Sometimes they go running or hike in Mission Trails Regional Park.

Nubs romps with his friends Bogey and Kublai. Nubs even goes to school. His trainer, Graham, gives him straight A's.

This small dog has done amazing things in his short life. He chose to travel 70 miles alone across a desert to be with Brian. It was a miracle he survived. The bigger miracle may be that this dog of war chose to become a dog of peace.

Now Nubs has a name and a person to call his own. And he shares the friendship and love he found with everyone he meets.

But Nubs saves his best kisses for his best buddy, Brian.

Howdy:

I can honestly tell you that when I met a special little dog with hardly any ears, I never could have guessed the journey he would take me on. Though we only saw each other every few weeks, he became my little buddy in Iraq. I started calling him Nubs, and the rest is history.

It's difficult for me to imagine how hard his life was in Iraq. He lived in a war zone, suffered abuse, and had to fight to stay alive. The fact that he would want anything to do with people after what he went through was amazing in itself. But defying all odds, he bonded with my entire team and lifted our spirits. He would make us laugh when things were tough and always made everyone smile. His incredible act of friendship and devotion is a testament to the bond between humans and animals. It also shows that if you do something kind for someone, dog or human, they will likely never forget it.

Nubs now resides with me in San Diego, California. He has it pretty good these days, going on hikes, running around the dog park, and playing with his friends Bogey and Kublai. He has adapted to life in the States, but I can't imagine how confusing the changes must have been for him. He doesn't seem to mind, though. Sometimes, it almost looks like he's smiling.

None of this could have been possible without the support of many amazing people. To everyone who donated and helped out—thank you from the bottom of my heart. Because of all of you, I have a friend for life.

Cheers,

Brian Dennis
San Diego, California

♥ Nubs! ♥

Nubs is a really amazing dog.

I'm glad th

I admire you.

Nubs is amazing because he

SCOOP!

an EXCLUSIVE by
MONTY MOLENSKI

additional words and pictures by
John Kelly and Cathy Tincknell

SCOOP!
THE DAILY ROAR
NO BULL! ROAR DEAL FOR EDITOR EXPOSED AS MEMBER OF THE "FAKE PERSON CLUB"
Top reporter Monty Molenski takes the bull by the horns!
THIS IS IT!
MY BIG CHANCE FOR A SCOOP!

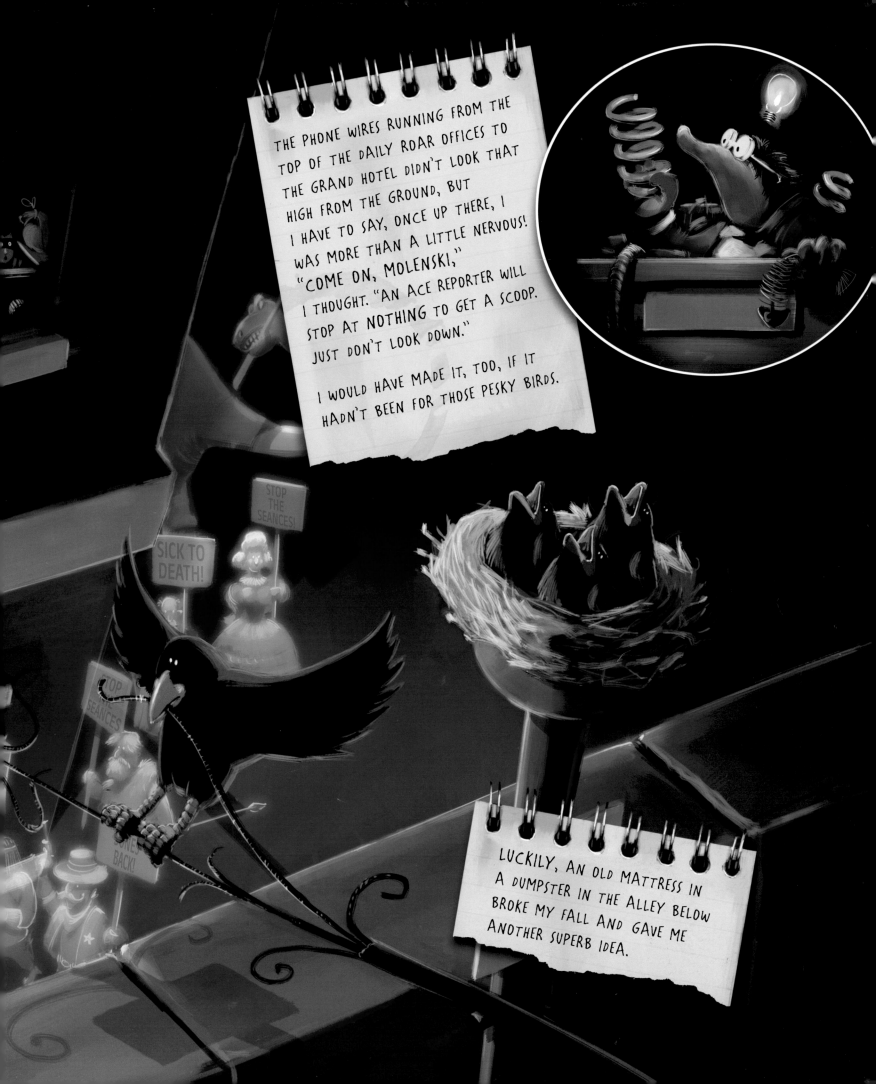

THE PHONE WIRES RUNNING FROM THE TOP OF THE DAILY ROAR OFFICES TO THE GRAND HOTEL DIDN'T LOOK THAT HIGH FROM THE GROUND, BUT I HAVE TO SAY, ONCE UP THERE, I WAS MORE THAN A LITTLE NERVOUS! "COME ON, MOLENSKI," I THOUGHT. "AN ACE REPORTER WILL STOP AT NOTHING TO GET A SCOOP. JUST DON'T LOOK DOWN."

I WOULD HAVE MADE IT, TOO, IF IT HADN'T BEEN FOR THOSE PESKY BIRDS.

LUCKILY, AN OLD MATTRESS IN A DUMPSTER IN THE ALLEY BELOW BROKE MY FALL AND GAVE ME ANOTHER SUPERB IDEA.

BACK ON THE ROOF OF THE DAILY
ROAR, I TOOK A DEEP BREATH AND
LAUNCHED MYSELF INTO SPACE
WEARING MY NEW "GRAVITY-DEFYING
MOLENSKI SPRING-BOOTS."
UNFORTUNATELY, THE SPRINGS WERE
RATHER MORE POWERFUL THAN I'D
CALCULATED. INSTEAD OF LANDING ON
THE ROOF OF THE GRAND HOTEL,
I OVERSHOT IT A BIT AND ALMOST
ENDED UP IN THE BOATING LAKE.

IT'S GOING TO BE A **LONG**
WALK BACK.

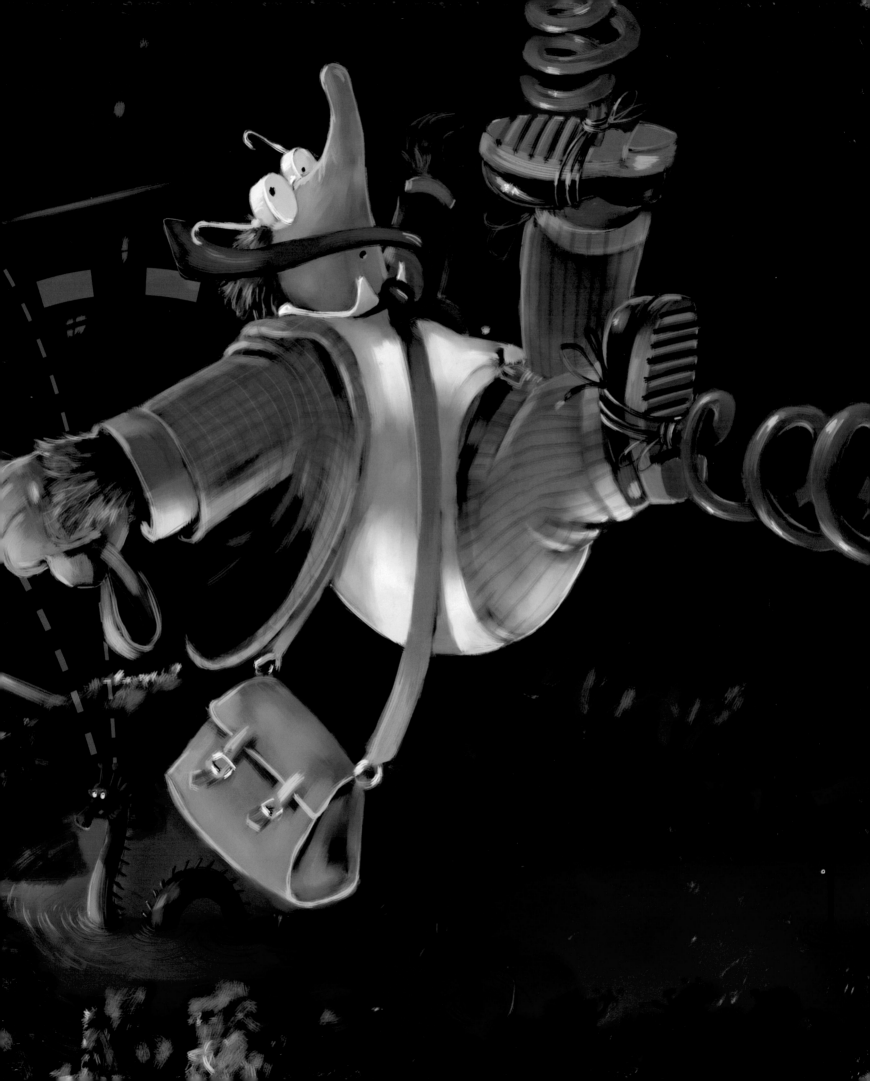

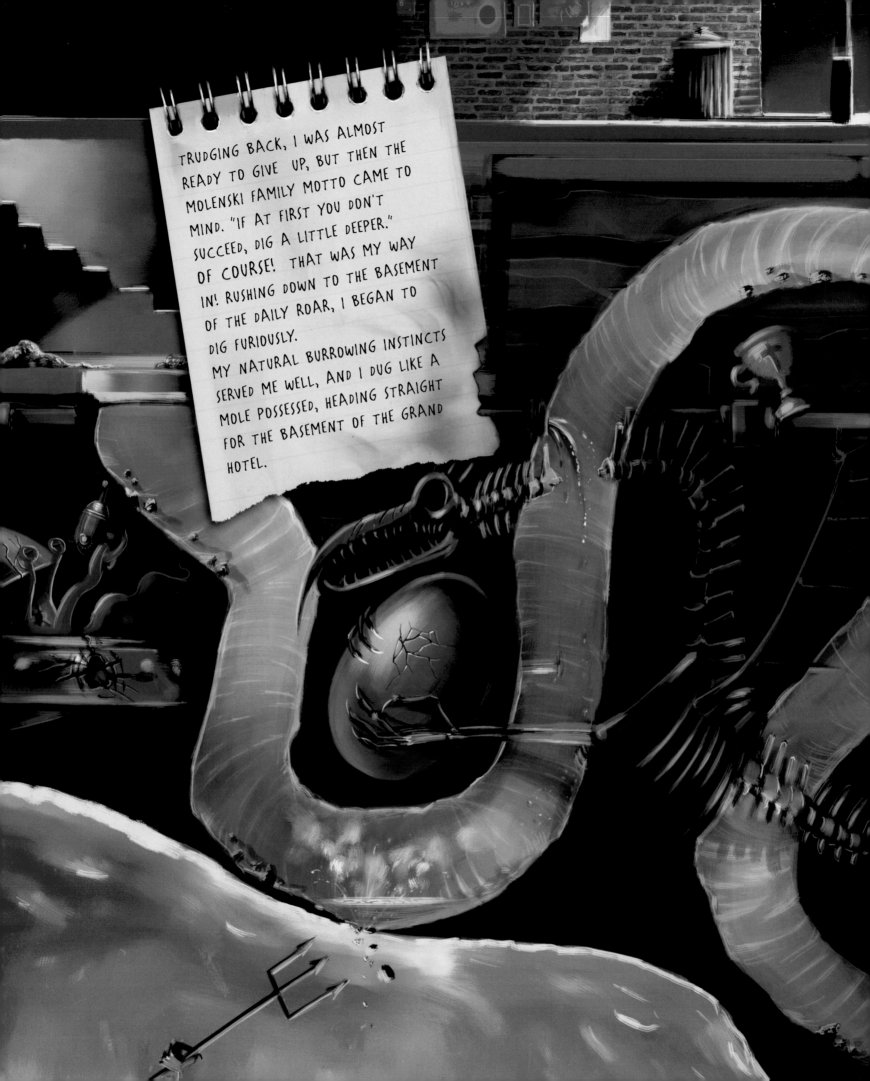

TRUDGING BACK, I WAS ALMOST READY TO GIVE UP, BUT THEN THE MOLENSKI FAMILY MOTTO CAME TO MIND. "IF AT FIRST YOU DON'T SUCCEED, DIG A LITTLE DEEPER." OF COURSE! THAT WAS MY WAY IN! RUSHING DOWN TO THE BASEMENT OF THE DAILY ROAR, I BEGAN TO DIG FURIOUSLY. MY NATURAL BURROWING INSTINCTS SERVED ME WELL, AND I DUG LIKE A MOLE POSSESSED, HEADING STRAIGHT FOR THE BASEMENT OF THE GRAND HOTEL.

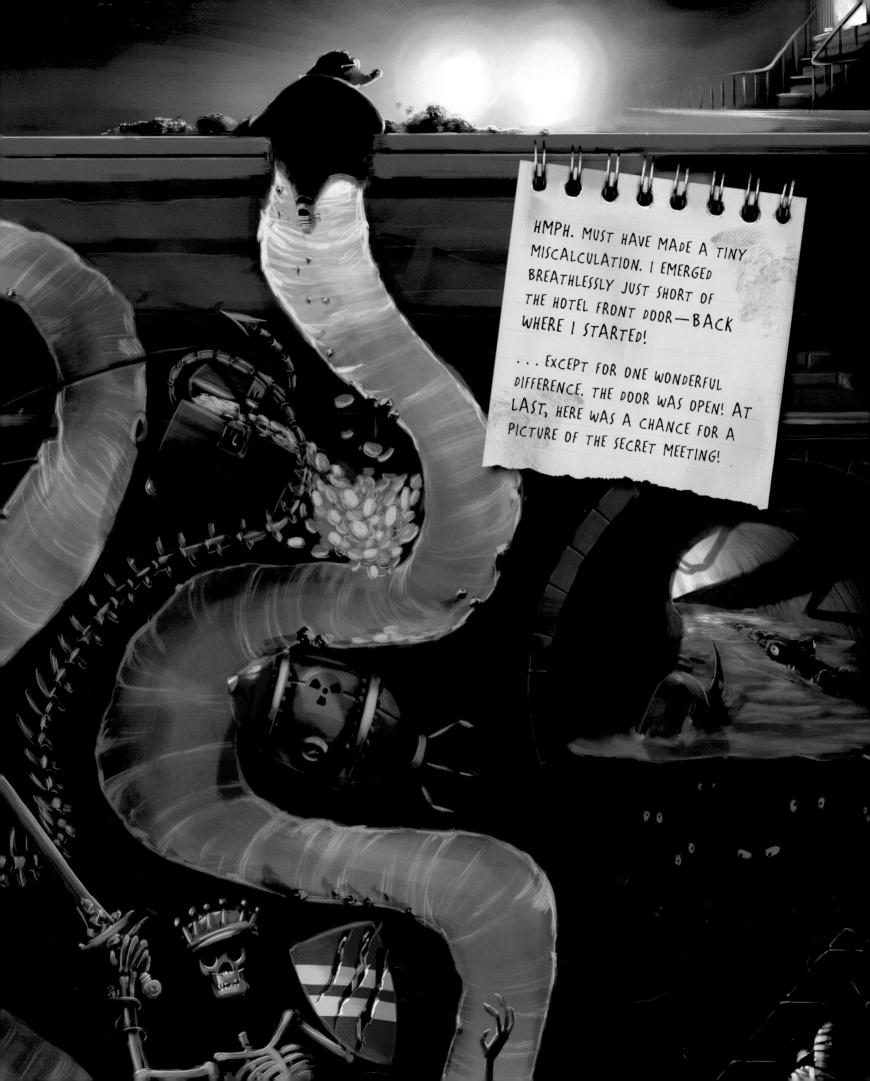

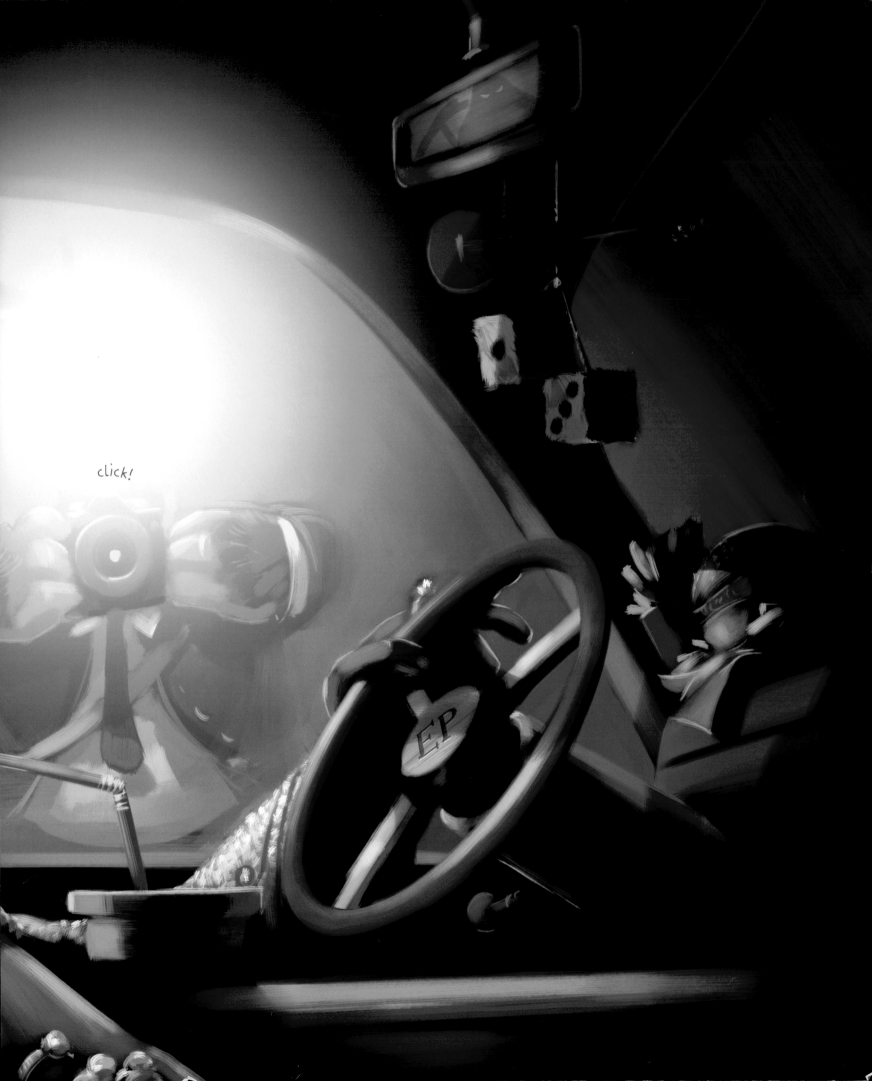

BY THE TIME THE CAR HAD PASSED BY,
THE ONLY PICTURE I COULD GET WAS OF
CHRIS CROC AND THE OTHER REPORTERS
LEAVING. NOT REALLY FRONT-PAGE
MATERIAL. WHAT HAD THEY BEEN UP
TO IN THERE?

THEN I SAW IT: MY CHANCE TO GET IN.
THE DOORMAN WAS DISTRACTED, THE
DOOR LEFT OPEN, AND WITH THE NIMBLE
SPEED OF A MOUNTAIN GOAT, I SNEAKED
IN BEHIND HIS BACK.

THE MYSTERY
IS ABOUT
TO BE SOLVED!

T PAGE CLUB

AH. THE FRONT PAGE CLUB.
SO THAT'S WHAT "F.P." STANDS FOR.

OH, DEAR.

DARKROOM
THE DAILY ROAR
ALL CAMERAS MUST BE LEFT HERE FOR OVERNIGHT PROCESSING
-THE NITE OWL
THOROUGHLY FED UP. RETURNED TO THE DESERTED DAILY ROAR OFFICES TO DROP OFF MY CAMERA AT THE NITE OWL'S FILM DEVELOPMENT LAB AS USUAL.
WHAT A WASTE OF TIME. OH, WELL. HOME TO BED.

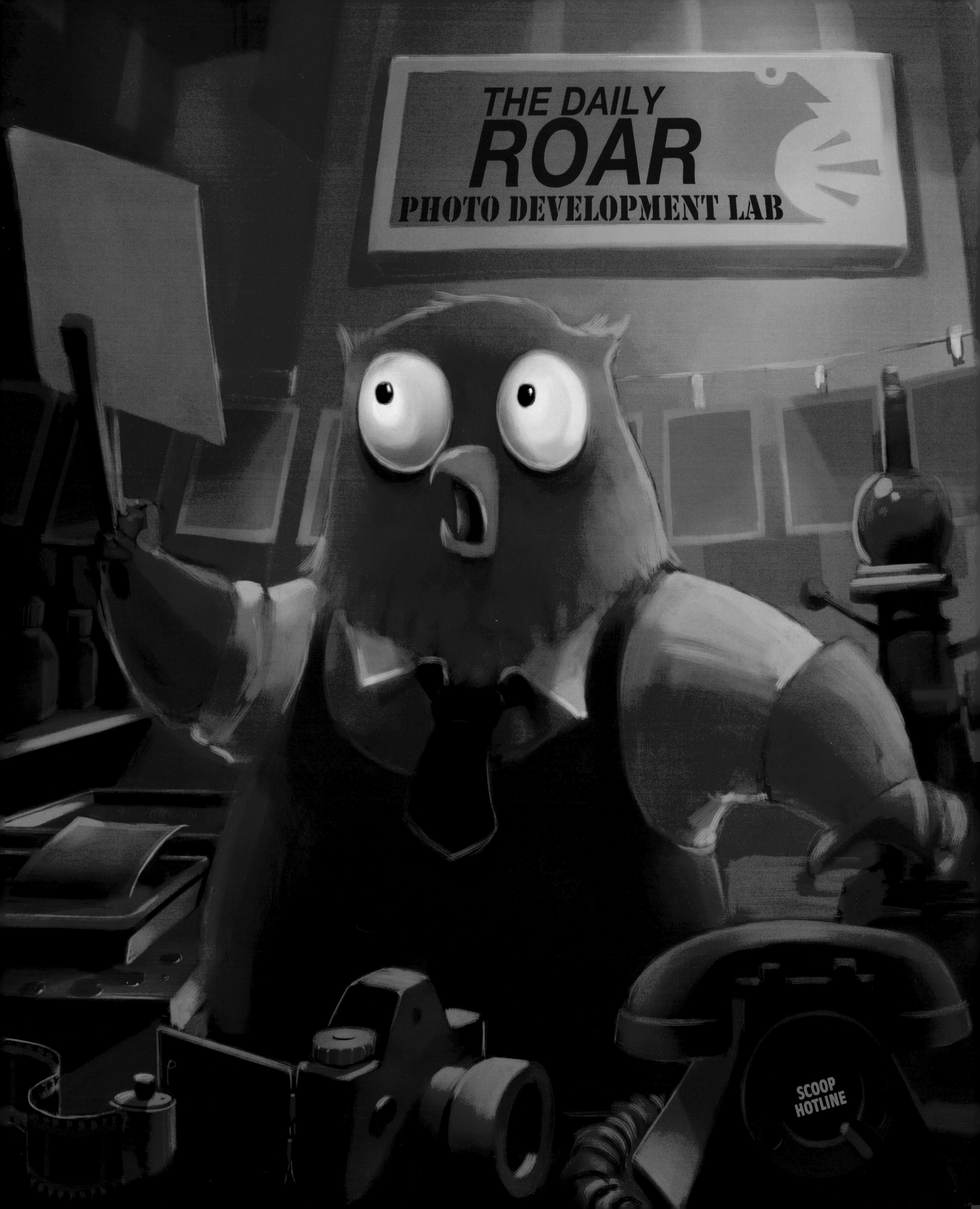
THE DAILY
ROAR
PHOTO DEVELOPMENT LAB
SCOOP
HOTLINE

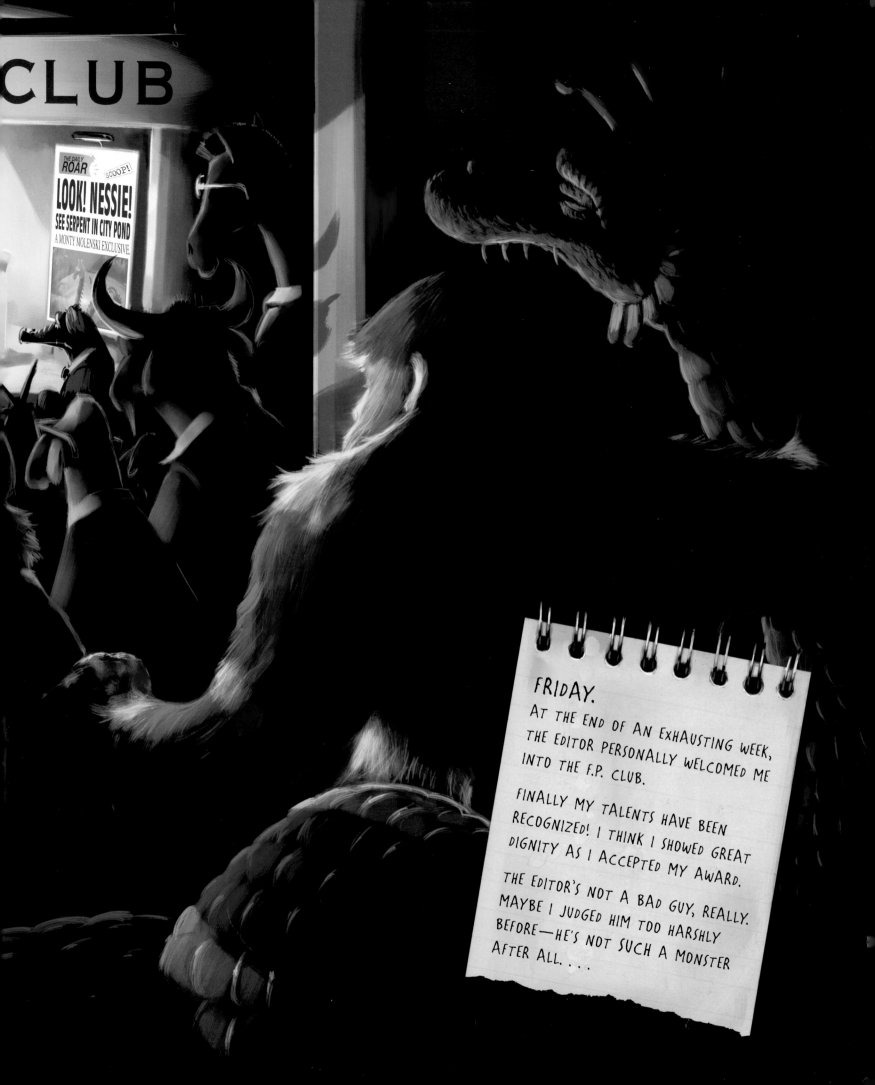

THE END?